Holy Shit!
Am I Really About to Graduate?

How to Get a Job Like a Boss

By Isaac Navias

Copyright © 2013 by Isaac Navias
All rights reserved.

Acknowledgements

I want to thank everyone who has helped me improve this book. A big thank you goes out to Matthew Soffietti, Lukas Hampton, Catherine Perkins, as well as my Mom and Dad for editing and contributing to my book. Thanks to Tim, Kelley, Sheng, Ruwan, Doug, and Tony for providing me with useful feedback. A big thanks to Tanya Stockton without whom I would have never written this book and I am grateful to Nancy Nguyen for introducing us. I also appreciate all the support and great marketing advice that I received from Melissa G Wilson. Thanks to everyone who made my college experience one of the greatest times of my life.

To my little brother and sister, I know you will find a way to get a hold of this book before you're old enough to read it... Just don't tell the parental units when you do!

Contents

Acknowledgements 2
Do I really have to graduate? Man, I love college! 5
The Stats 8
Who is this Dude? 10
The Online Application Process (Finding the Diamond in the Rough) 11
Don't Be Afraid to Get Rejected 16
The Referral Program 18
    Volunteering 20
    Internships 21
    Professors 21
    Academic Advisors 22
    Social and Professional Fraternities 23
    Clubs 24
    The Informational Interview 25
    Networking 26
    Klepto Isaac 27
    Networking with the Family 29
    We all "Sell" 31
How You Can Help Me 33
LinkedIn 35
Creative Thinking & Tampons 40
Using College Resources 42
    Career Resource Center: 42
    Resume/CV reviews: 42
    Help with Interviewing: 43
    Mentoring program: 43
    Job and Internship Listing: 43
    Job Fairs: 44
    Stand out! 44
    Review 46
Magic 48
EQ 50
The Interview 52
Creating your own Job 62
Extra Resources 65
Endnotes 67

Do I really have to graduate?
Man, I love college!

College is a special time but wow does it go quickly. It starts out innocently enough. Playing the Mario Kart drinking game during freshman year (two shots for last place, one shot for third place... it gets ugly quick -- you start losing, you keep losing!). To pulling all nighters in the lobby to make sure you do well on your calc exam.

We even had epic battles. During my freshman year, both Mom and Dad sent me huge Easter baskets. I ended up with over 50 Peeps. I tried hard to give them away. But, no dice, since Peeps are, well, gross. We didn't want to throw the Peeps out; it's no good to waste them.

So my roommate and I started the Peep Wars. One day while doing homework I looked over at Rich. We made eye contact. I handed him a couple Peeps and we went running into our friends' room to chuck Peeps at them. The Peep Wars were born.

For the next two weeks, Rich and I would grab more Peeps, run into a random room and start throwing them. People started saving my Peeps and throwing them back at us. The battle of the 4th floor was the biggest: there were fifteen people in the hall throwing Peeps in an epic battle of wit and courage.

Fast forward to senior year. It's 3am and I'm lying in my bed about to go to sleep. Then I hear my roommate knocking at my door. The conversation went something like this:

Brodie: "We got to make the Facebook group for the party!"

Me: "Dude, it's 3am. Let's just do it tomorrow."

Brodie: "Stop being a fuckin' noob, we got to do it now. We need a theme."

Me: "I don't know, man. Let's make it a hat party."

Brodie: "Ya! That's awesome! And we need a prize for the winner."

Me: "Well, let's make the winner a ham sandwich."

Brodie: "Hell ya, people will love that!"

And people did. Never underestimate the power a ham sandwich has on drunk people. We set up a run-way and everything. Over 40 hats were displayed.

The winner tried (and failed) to pull a back flip out of a Kan Jam (if you don't know what this is google it and buy one). He won a toasted ham and cheese sandwich. The top 3 received ham sandwiches. Blair, who came in fourth, is still upset to this day that she didn't get one.

Then it suddenly hits you...

"Holy shit I am four months away from graduating and I have no clue what I am doing."

You start stressing out, or you push it out of your mind. You know this economy is real tough, but you have learned so much; there must be a job out there. Most college students start doing the same thing around this point. They get online and start applying for jobs.

I know how it feels. I applied to over 50 jobs when that *holy shit* moment hit me. I thought to myself, "I'm in the top 5% of my class, I have great extracurricular activities, I'll get a call back."

Several weeks later...nothing. Several weeks more and I have applied to another 50 jobs...nothing.

That's when you start to panic and get discouraged. Your friends around you are giving up left and right. Most plan on going to grad school or move in with their parents after they leave college. "There are no jobs out there," they say.

Well let me tell you something. THEY ARE WRONG. There are jobs out there, and while you are in college you have amazing resources available to you provided by your university. Trust me, it gets MUCH harder to get a job a year after college. Colleges want you to get a job. At graduation, students with jobs are a huge statistic that all colleges advertise. Plus, if you have a job, you have money to donate to the university.

In this book we will look at the different resources all colleges offer to their students and how to use them. We will look at how the online application process has changed everything and explore the statistics of who is getting hired and why most people are failing to get call backs. We will look at networking, interviewing, applying, using social media, and getting **SEEN** in a mass of jobless Americans.

The Stats

So why should you read this book? Let's look at some scary-ass statistics.

The unemployment rate for Millenials (Americans aged 18 to 29) is higher than any other age group.

In 2012, about 1.5 million, or 53.6 percent, of bachelor's degree-holders under the age of 25 last year were jobless or underemployed: the highest share in at least 11 years.[1]

In the last year, new graduates were more likely to be employed as waiters, waitresses, bartenders and food-service helpers than as engineers, physicists, chemists and mathematicians combined (100,000 versus 90,000). There were more new grads working in office-related jobs such as receptionists or payroll clerks than in all computer professional jobs (163,000 versus 100,000).

Broken down by occupation, young college graduates were heavily represented in jobs that require a high school diploma or less. Slightly over half of new graduates end up getting a job that does not require a college diploma.

"Students from the Class of 2008 and later faced a significantly bleaker future than grads from prior years, according to the study. Less than half were able to find jobs within one year of graduation, down from 73% before 2008." [2]

Now not only are you competing against the new graduates in your graduating class, but you could also be competing against 50% of the graduates from 2008 on since about 50% of graduates since 2008 are jobless or underemployed.

Now that you've shat yourself, wipe yourself off and let's do this -- don't worry, I'll wait.

The purpose of this book is to help you become one of the 50% who gets the job you want in a field you enjoy.

Who is this Dude?

Let me tell you a little about my career experience since college. I was hired right out of college to be an Executive HR (Human Resources) for Target. Over 350 people were interviewed, but only 2 of us were hired.

At age 22 I oversaw 100 team members, making a salary of $50,000+ a year. I interviewed over 300 people and hired over 50 team members for positions ranging from cashier to senior team leaders.

From this experience I have learned the secrets about the hiring and interviewing process. Due to my successful screening techniques I ranked #1 in my district for hiring on-time and retaining new hires.

After I left Target I created my own consulting company focused on helping small entrepreneurs succeed. I have helped several clients screen and hire employees.

In this book I will give you insights into how HRs make their hiring decisions.

This book is written for college students, not their parents (like most other career books). I am only 3 years out of college and still have my college experience fresh in my mind.

This book is short, but game-changing. Let's Start!

The Online Application Process
(Finding the Diamond in the Rough)

The transition from handing in paper applications to the online application process has changed everything. In my opinion, it has changed everything for the worse, for both applicants and hiring decision makers (HRs).

In the old days you had to spend 15 minutes to an hour to fill out each application. Then you had to go and actually drop it off at the company. This ensured that the jobs you were applying for were ones you really wanted. You also had a good chance of talking to the HR when you dropped off your application (which significantly increased your chances of getting an interview).

Now you can apply to 20 jobs in about 10 minutes if you are using a program like Monster or Career Builder. People can apply to jobs with the click of a button, even if they are not a good fit, because it's so easy. You may say, "Well if I can apply to 20 jobs in 10 minutes instead of 20 jobs in 10 hours -- doesn't that help me??!" The answer is **NO**.

Let's look at it from the HR point of view. HR's are getting 20-100 applications *a day*, compared to the 1 or 2 they used to get. Over half of those applications are from people who are not qualified or don't want the job. HR's have to spend so much more time mining though applications, and HR's can tell almost nothing useful from them.

Not only that, but HR's in this economy are being asked to take on more business responsibilities even while their hours are getting cut. They do not have time to look though the ridiculous amount of applications they are receiving. While before you might have been in a pool of 100 applicants, you are now going up against 1,000-10,000 applicants.

Studies have shown that only 20% of hires come from applications. People with tons of experience are applying for the same job you are because they have been laid off. Your application next to theirs is going to be thrown out entirely due to your lack of experience. So your chance of being seen (if all you do is submit your application online) is next to nothing.

The other big negative is that because of the online application process, your interaction with the HR or hiring decision maker has disappeared. Before, when you dropped your application off, you would talk to the HR, or at least an employee. Now there is no interaction. As an HR I can tell quite accurately within 2 minutes of talking to someone if they will be a good fit for the job. Here's a real story about how I hired my Senior Team Leader when I was at Target.

The Sr. TL is a high position at Target, only one slot under Executive. All Sr. TLs are expected to move up to the Executive position within 2 years. The HR before me had been looking for a Sr. TL for over 6 months before I took over. I made hiring one a priority soon after I started. After a month of searching I still had no success finding someone to fill this position.

One day I got called up to the front of the store because someone asked to speak to me **by name**. This piqued my curiosity, so I went to the front and spoke to this young man. He was in his early 20s and he had a pitch ready for me.

He told me he had studied Target at college and was determined to get a management position, even if he had to start as a cashier.

After 2 minutes of talking to him, I knew we would hire him -- probably for a higher-up position.

I told him he would have to apply online before we could interview him, and he said he already had. That surprised me because I had been looking at every application for a TL spot. So I called my TLs in to interview him on the spot while I looked up his application.

I thought maybe my assistant had turned his application down (my assistant did the first review of most applications because I did not have time to). When I found his application (in the rejection folder) I was surprised to see it was me that hadn't passed him onto the next stage. I had rejected it because he had put in limited availability and he didn't stand out on paper.

Well, we hired him as a Sr. TL and he was promoted to Executive within 6 months. The crazy thing is, if he had not come in and asked for me by name, he would never even have gotten a call back.

This experience taught me a few things about applying to any company:

1. **Always put open availability.**

Even if that is not the case -- you can explain what it really is in the interview -- you will not get an interview if you don't put open availability. HRs have a time limit for how long an application can sit in the first stage. The easiest way to knock people out or move them to the next stage is if they have open availability.

2. **If you really want a job, make sure you talk to the HR.**

Most HRs are like me and can quickly identify if you have the skills to succeed just by talking to you. However, most companies have standard applications you have to fill out and they give HR's next to no good info. Going in and talking to the HR in person is by far the best approach. This also shows the HR that you are serious about the job. Calling can work, but is not as effective. Make sure if you are calling you have the HRs name and a 30 second pitch ready.

3. **Always ask for the HR or hiring manager by name.**

This is *very* important. I would get over 10 calls a day from people asking about their application. I didn't have time for that so I screened all my calls. If they called and asked about their application or asked to talk to the HR, they would get my secretary or the front desk. However, if they asked for me by name I would take the call.

If that young man had just asked to talk to the HR, I probably would have sent out my secretary to talk to him instead. So how do you find out the name of the HR? There are many different ways:

> <> Look it up on the company's website. Many companies will have their management positions listed on their website.

> <> Look it up on LinkedIn. We will explore the use of LinkedIn in a future chapter. This can be a great way to find more info about the HR.

> <> Alternatively, just go into the company and ask an employee! "Hi, I'm really interested in getting a job here. Can you tell me the name of your HR?"

4. Have an elevator pitch ready when to you talk to the HR.

Many people would call and say, "Hi, I am checking on my application." My response: "Ok, congratulations, I'll look at it later." (I never would.) You need to have a pitch ready to set you apart from all the others. This pitch should be 30 seconds to 1 minute for a phone call and 1 to 2 minutes when talking to the HR in person. This pitch needs to focus on how you can benefit THEM (the company). Not how much you want the job, or what your qualifications are. Hiring decision-makers want to know how you are going to help the company.

For example, if I was to apply for an HR position, my pitch would be: "Hi, I am interested in working for your company. I know you will benefit from me being the HR because I am good at quickly and accurately identifying people's skill sets and whether they would be a good fit. This allows me to reduce the amount of time the company is spending interviewing as well as increase the quality of new hires. I am also great with people and am able to get employees to work to the best of their ability due to my leadership skills. This will increase productivity of the workers you currently have and increase revenue."

BOOM. 30 seconds and I have given them 2 ways I will benefit THEM.

Let's recap:

1. Only 20% of hires come from people who have just applied online. This number is worse for new grads because you will lose to people who have more experience than you. Don't get discouraged when you don't get a call back. Just realize that the system doesn't work and you need to try a different approach.

2. Go into the company and ask to speak to the HR by name.

3. Have a pitch ready about how you can help them. Even if you have applied online, bring in your resume to hand to them. A paper application will sit on the desk and force the HR to look at it.

We will talk more about how to get your application seen, but first let's take a journey back to senior year.

Don't Be Afraid to Get Rejected

It is important that you recognize that sometimes you will not get call backs or have successful interviews. I have seen too many people miss out on a job they really want just because they are so afraid of being rejected. Not getting a call back is not that big of a deal. Not getting a job because you never applied is a much bigger deal.

During my senior year, my roommate, Ruwan, and I were both afraid of approaching and getting rejected by girls. We decided that we would overcome our fears and learn how to approach women. We found out quite quickly that we were not actually bad at it; we were just doing a couple of things wrong and had not tried for a while. I learnt a life truth during this adventure.

If you are unwilling to fail you will never succeed.

We stopped worrying about if we "failed" and started focusing on having fun.

I honestly don't remember how the idea started. Somehow we ended up having Styrofoam cups at our house after hosting a party. We started talking about how we used to play telephone with those types of cups. We decided to make an old school telephone by connecting 2 Styrofoam cups with a 3-foot-long string. Later that night, we went out to the bar with our telephone to attempt to approach a couple girls in a way they would never forget.

We got to the bar and I wandered over to two girls who were at the bar.

"Hey," I said. "My friend and I were arguing about this question and I wanted to get your opinion; What is your favorite drinking holiday?"

I soon had them talking and laughing. After about 2 minutes Ruwan walked up behind me and tapped me on the shoulder.

"Excuse me," I said to the girls. "I need to take this."

I grabbed the cup he handed me and put it to my ear. Ruwan, standing about 3 feet away, said into his cup: "Tell her she smells nice."

"You smell nice," I said to the girl on the left.

"Put your arm around her waist," said Ruwan.

"How you doing?" I said, sliding my arm around her waist.

The girl on the right turned to Ruwan. "I can see you."

With a completely straight face Ruwan answered, "Excuse me, Miss, I am in the middle of a conversation," and went back to talking into the cup.

At this point everyone was laughing. I introduced myself and Ruwan.

"Hi, you may have seen me before. I'm that guy that was talking into the cup."

(And, yes, we did get their numbers.)

BTW, in case you need to see what NOT to do (HIMYM clip): http://www.youtube.com/watch?v=ya4R4LzL4Iw

The lesson here is to find ways to overcome your fear of rejection. If you want a good job out of college, prepare to be rejected many times before you succeed. If you let your fear of rejection prevent you from applying, you will never succeed. Try to add in creative ways of approaching companies that will make the experience more enjoyable for you.

17

The Referral Program

Being referred to a company is one of the most effective ways to go about getting a job. As I explained before, HRs are swamped with applications and looking for a way to narrow down the field without losing the gems. One effective way that almost all companies now use is the employee referral program. Most companies have rewards for an employee who refers an applicant that gets hired. HRs will also go out of their way to call in applicants that were referred by a current employee. Why? Let's look at some data.

Society for Human Resource Management (SHRM) found that around 24% of employees hired came from a referral. Many studies have found this number is even higher. OK, so 24% is not that much higher than 20% (those who get hired from just applying online). True, but there is one big difference. Only 6.4% of the applicants are those who were referred. If 6.4% of the applicants are getting 24% of the hires you can see how powerful getting referred can be.

Dr. John Sullivan, an HR thought leader, looked at the numbers behind why referrals are quickly becoming the highest source of new hires. The statistics I list here are from his article "10 Compelling Numbers That Reveal the Power of Employee Referrals."[3]

It may be startling to some that referrals are now the #1 source in hiring volume, as well as #1 for new hire quality. People hired who were referred have the highest retention rate after one year (46% compared to 33% from job boards).

Dr. Sullivan found that while referrals are only 6.9% of applicants, top-performing firms hire referrals for 46% of job openings. Let's look at that a different way. For top-performing firms, 1 out of 3 applicants hired is a referral, while the average applicant-to-hire ratio was 1:18. **That means you have a 600% higher chance of getting hired by a top company if you are referred.**

So why are companies, especially top-performing companies, focusing on hiring referrals? Well we touched on one point: they have a much higher retention rate. Also, data shows that hires from a well-designed referral program have the highest job performance of any recruiting source.

A good referral program also saves a ton of management time because it greatly reduces time spent advertising and interviewing. Studies also show that time-to-initial-productivity is much higher for those who were referred. Good referral programs help the management connect with their employees and lets them have a voice on who is getting hired. Looking at the numbers we can now understand why companies are focusing so much on referrals.

So why did I share all of these numbers with you? First off, it was to show the drastic increase in the chances of getting hired by being referred. You can see why by understanding the benefits to the company. So now that we KNOW that getting referred is so wickedly important to getting hired how do we go about getting referred? There are many ways that we will cover in this book.

Volunteering can be a key way to network with the goal of getting referred. Look up the volunteer organizations that the company you are interested in works with.

LinkedIn can be another great way to find connections you already have with the company, as well as help you find new connections.

Using other forms of **Social Media** (Facebook, Twitter) can be effective for finding connections that you already have previously weren't aware of.

Informational interviews with professionals can be a great way to network, as well as provide valuable information.

Getting involved in **clubs or fraternities** at school can give you connections to alumni.

Even **networking with family members** can give you a big edge.

Also, remember that you don't need to know a person super well in order to ask them to refer you. I have been referred to companies by people I have never met (a girl that was in a LinkedIn group with me), or that I have only met once (at a place I volunteered). Most companies have a reward program for employees who refer someone who is hired, so as long as the employee has a good vibe from you they won't have a problem referring you.

There are a lot of ways to help yourself get referred. Let's take a closer look at the most efficient and successful strategies.

Volunteering

Volunteering can be an EXCELLENT way to go about getting a job. It can help you connect to a specific industry as well as allow you to do some good in your community. I have gotten an internship, a business partnership, and my first client all from volunteering. My internship came while I was doing community service as part of my fraternity.

We were working at a business that was basically a Salvation Army for houses (used doors, windows, tools, etc). I got to talking to one of the employees and was telling him about how I was looking for an internship in the green industry. Out of the blue he suggested that I contact Bill over at Rubber Form because they were looking for interns. Hence my internship in the field that I wanted to be in.

Using volunteering to get a job can be quite effective. First take a look at what volunteer opportunities are available to you in your area. You want to pick one that is in your field. There are a variety of volunteer finders out there.

The federal government operates Serve.gov, which provides an overview and a volunteer finder powered by All for Good. Other good websites to visit include VolunteerMatch, idealist.org, Points of Light, AmeriCorps, and AARP's Create the Good program. United Way is also a great volunteer organization that has volunteer centers and offices all over the country. When looking for a place to volunteer, pick a place that matches your industry and an organization that you will enjoy working for. To really get the benefits of networking from volunteer work you will need to actually do good volunteer work first.

Build up trust and friendship in the organization before you start asking about jobs. Also, volunteering in your industry can give you great experience, which will help you get noticed on your resume and in your interview. Volunteering, especially in this economy, may be the most effective way to get a job. Plus, you get to do good in your community!

Internships

Internships can turn into jobs. Some majors will require internships so you can get "real world" experience. But, an internship can also be like an extended job interview. The company is observing and evaluating you and, if they like what they see, they may offer you a job (or even create one for you). Even if there is no immediate job, you are still on their radar for future opportunities. You also make connections during internships. The relationship you have with your Internship Supervisor is especially important. They can help you explore the field you are interested in and assist you in making connections. Also, remember to get that all-important recommendation letter from them before you leave the internship as well as permission to use them as a reference for future jobs.

Professors

Professors are a great tool to use when looking for a job. They are quite connected and respected in the community. They can help you network your way into a job. It is worth your time to create good relationships with professors you respect. Creating a good relationship with a professor is also key for that ever-so-important letter of recommendation. If you're about to graduate, hopefully you have made a favorable impression on at least one professor.

Sometimes students are intimidated by professors or don't think they are interested in them. So I asked a professor and assistant dean about the best way to build a good relationship with professors. Her advice follows:

1. Visit during their office hours and show your interest in doing well in their class.

2. Find out about their interests (read their profile online and check out articles and/or books they have written) and get them talking about it (not usually that hard!).

3. Ask if they need any assistance with their research or other projects they are working on.

4. Check to see if they have a LinkedIn account (many colleges encourage faculty to set up accounts). This can also help you see other people that the professor may be able to help you connect to.

Academic Advisors

Sometimes, your academic advisor is a faculty member but they may also be professional staff members. Either way, they are important resources. Depending on your college's system, your academic advisor may know you the best if they have been advising you for several years. In addition to working with you while you are in college to prepare for a career, they are also good resources for recommendation letters, referrals and connections to other influential people in academia and the community. Get to know them and let them get to know you (show up at times besides advising appointments to talk about your interests and future) so they can provide even more individualistic advice and assistance. Also, don't be afraid to request a specific academic advisor that may have similar interests, or who you feel you may be able to connect with on a more personal level.

Social and Professional Fraternities

Yes, fraternities often get a bad name because of the drinking and hazing that are sometimes associated with them. In reality, it depends on which fraternity you join and what the chapter in your college is like. There are many studies that show that joining a fraternity can have a great impact on your future success.

Some startling stats about fraternity members are:

> <> Nationally, 71% of all fraternity and sorority members graduate, while only 50% of non-members graduate.[4]

> <> The overall fraternity and sorority GPA is higher than the overall collegiate GPA.

> <> Since 1910, 85% of the Supreme Court Justices have been fraternity or sorority members.

> <> 85% of the Fortune 500 key executives are fraternity or sorority members.

> <> Since 1825, all but three U.S. presidents have been members of a fraternity.[5]

When picking a fraternity you need to look at a couple things. The first one is: what is your goal?

If your goal is to get a job and network, then you want to look for a fraternity that is national and has strong alumni members. Most times people just look at how big the frat is on campus, but in reality what matters more is how many alumni there are.

There is an increasing amount of professional fraternities popping up. These can be extremely valuable in teaching you real life skills while you're in college as well as helping you network outside of college.

My Fraternity, Alpha Kappa Psi, is the largest Professional Business Fraternity in the world with over 240,000 members worldwide. Since leaving college I have gotten interviews, clients, and friends from AKPsi members I had never met before. The networking I have been able to do since I became an AKPsi Alumni has been incredible and it is a major reason for my networking success.

I do want to warn you about off-campus fraternities; they have been kicked off campus for a reason and are usually just party frats. I had several friends flunk out of college because they joined an off-campus fraternity.

If you do have a couple years of college left, I highly recommend you look into what fraternities/sororities are on campus and see whether it is worth the time and effort you need to put in to join. A good friend once told me, "Pledging is the most fun you will never want to have again."

Clubs

Colleges have tons of clubs that can teach you a lot more about the real world than formal education. Many clubs are a lot like fraternities since many have a national presence. They, like frats, can create excellent networking opportunities, both in and out of college.

Clubs differ from frats because they can be joined immediately, and often relate directly to the career you are interested in. Even if you only have a semester left, go out and check what clubs would be worth joining.

Most colleges have clubs associated with a certain major. I was part of SHRM (an HR club). My roommate was in a financial club. Another friend was in an industrial engineering club. Look to see if there's a club associated with your major/job interest. Check it out. Many times these clubs will have connections in the community. They will also bring in guest speakers related to the industry, giving you the chance to network with these speakers. Asking them for an informational interview after their speech can be a great networking tactic.

The Informational Interview

One of the key reasons to join clubs/fraternities is because they often will bring in professional speakers. This can be a great opportunity for you to network and get a referral. One of the best ways to network with a speaker is to ask them for an informational interview after they are done giving their speech.

What is it?

An informational interview is when you interview someone who is an expert in their field with the goal of obtaining more information about that field.

Why do it?

This is a great way to get one-on-one time with a professional. It is also a fantastic way to network with high-end professionals.

How do I ask for one?

Let's say a speaker came to your class and you wanted to network with this person and find out more information about their field. If you go up and ask them if you can do an informational interview with them, you will almost always get it. People love to talk about themselves and their fields of expertise. They are even more excited about it when they are talking to a young adult who is genuinely interested in what they have to say.

What do I ask during an informational interview?

First you need to define your goal. Is your goal to get a job, or just to find out more about the industry? You have to tailor your questions to your goal.

I like to start by asking them how they got into that industry, to get them talking about themselves.

You can ask which key skills you need to be successful, what's the salary you can expect, and secrets to getting into the industry.

One question I always ask is what books they would recommend reading!

What do I do after the interview?

Thank them for their time and ask them for their business card/email. Send them a thank-you note for meeting with you within a day or two. Add them on LinkedIn.

By doing this informational interview you have now added a professional to your network. I have received several interviews by asking people I did info interviews with to help me get an interview with their company. I have also learned secrets about industries I was interested in learning more about. Overall the informational interview can be a great way for you to network with professionals that you would otherwise have a hard time connecting with.

Networking

So I have shown how the online application process is a broken system. I have also shown you how to overcome that broken system by getting referred. I've given you different tools for you to network your way into a referral. So let's talk about networking for a second.

I am sure you have heard about the importance of networking over and over. Well, those people aren't lying, but they don't really tell you what networking is.

Networking is just meeting new people with the goal of creating a mutually beneficial relationship between 2 people.

One of the keys to good networking is to first look at how you can help them. If you can help someone out with something they will instantly join your network. Successful networking is about mutual gains between people.

Another key is to always be networking. Just talking about what you do/want to do will help you network. The other day I was getting a deep tissue massage and the masseuse asked me what I did for a living. I told him some of what I do, and I strategically talked about how I help clients increase their online presence (one of the many consulting services I offer). All I did was talk about it and at the end of the massage he asked about hiring me. Now I have a new client.

Not once did I try to sell my service. All I did was identify where I could help him the most and spoke about it.

Networking can happen anywhere, and once you start networking you will be shocked at the connections you make at the most times and random places. Many times the best networking happens in social settings, not business settings. More networking happens over drinks than anywhere else.

Klepto Isaac

One day I was hanging out with friends in my room and suddenly I had the urge to go Questing. I turned to my friend Nicole and said "I'm going to go on a Quest, check you later." As I left my room I realized my quest was to acquire as many things as possible.

The first thing I did was visit the room across the hall. I remember going into the girl's room and trying to steal her lamp. For some reason I couldn't pick it up. I kept trying to grab it, but the lamp kept tugging back at me. Her boyfriend was lying on her bed watching me. He held out his hand in a stop signal and said, "Isaac, Isaac, Isaac! Hold on!"

He then slowly reached down, unplugged the lamp, and quickly said, "Gogogogo!"

It was then I found out that for some reason people love to help you steal stuff.

Next I decided to venture into a wild new land AKA the dorm next to mine. I quickly recruited one of my buddies, Albert, who lived there, to help me. So I started going into different rooms and taking random things like posters and cologne. A random kid stopped me and was like, "Hey, what are you doing?"

I told him I was stealing random stuff and he said, "Cool, I'll keep an eye out for you."

I couldn't believe it.

I ended up in Kelly's room, a party acquaintance. Albert and I came up with an elaborate plan to steal their rug. They knew something was up considering that I was carrying 2 lamps, a couple posters and a bottle of cologne (which I had taken from Albert's room without his knowledge). Albert, using his Asian Charm, convinced them we weren't going to do anything and got them to step off their floor run. As soon as they did, Albert and I grabbed her rug and bolted.

I woke up the next morning and I was looking around. There were a bunch of new lamps, some new posters, and the rug (which looked great in the middle of our room). Then my roommate woke up. "Hey Isaac," he said. "I really like it, but where the fuck did that rug come from??"

The next day I posted on Facebook: Hey friends... If I visited you last night and you're now missing something, I probably have it in my room. Stop by and say hi.

I had friends stopping by all day.

"Hey, do you have my light?"

"...Yea, it's over there."

The rug, however, stayed in our room for about a month. I wouldn't give it to the girls until they played Apples to Apples with us. They did eventually come and play an epic game of Apples to Apples that was the foundation of our friendship. So I used my silly questing to network and make new friends.

I am still good friends with both Kelly and Blair to this day and Kelly has helped me in my career several times already. See -- always be networking!

Networking with the Family

One of the best ways new grads are getting jobs is though networking though their family. Trust me, I get the feeling that you want to be independent and make your own way, but there is no shame in asking your family for help.

Your parents have been alive a lot longer than you and have built up a bigger network than you. I had several friends who got good jobs right out of college by utilizing their parents' networks. One friend got a job because he was playing basketball with his dad and his dad's friends and mentioned he was looking for a job. His dad's friend got him into his company to get an interview and he got hired making over $40,000 a year right out of college.

I strongly encourage you to talk to your parents about what you want to do when you leave college and ask them if they have anyone in their network that could help you. Reach out to grandparents, aunts, and uncles and ask them the same question. Make sure you ask specific questions. Many times family members want to help, but don't know how to best help you. Asking "Do you know anyone who works at Google?" will be much more effective than saying, "I'm looking for a job. Can you help?"

Even while writing this book, I was helped by using my parents' network. I got a meeting with the assistant director of alumni programs in the Career Services Center at Syracuse University because I asked my mom (who works at SU) to do an email introduction with her. In this economy it matters much more who you know than what you know! So, adding your parents/family's network to who you know gives you a much better chance at finding a job that you want. Do not be ashamed of needing help from your family. In this economy our generation needs as much help as we can get so don't lose this huge resource over pride.

We all "Sell"

The following chapter on selling was contributed by Lukas Hampton

Sales, sell and salesperson are words most people HATE! But believe it or not, this is something we do every day and should LOVE! Being able to sell yourself and your services is key in networking and getting hired.

So what does selling yourself really mean? All it means is having the ability to leave a lasting impression on someone that shows them the VALUE in YOU as a person.

Typically, the FIRST impression is the most important. When someone meets you, the first impression sets the bar that every conversation thereafter is filtered through. Most people think about a few things when they first meet you: Am I feeling good talking to this person right now? What am I gaining from this conversation? How much of my time should I spend with this person? What valuable qualities does this person have? Remember that your VALUE is what will set you apart from others, and the ability to "Sell" yourself will determine whether or not you can guide a person to understanding that value in you.

Your own value as a person, is not something I can tell you about yourself. It is a discovery you must find within your own being. I will, however, touch briefly on three qualities I have found that most successful people I know value and appreciate in others they surround themselves with.

Number one, is good communication skills. Having good communication skills has more to do with being a good listener than anything else. Rather than thinking about what you'll say next to respond to someone, listen. REALLY listen to what they are saying. You may have heard the saying "God gave you two ears and one mouth use them appropriately." I believe you'll find, when you start using them in those proportions in which you have them, your conversations will be much more interactive and wholesome. While listening you can also learn what the other person values in a person. That gives you a cheat sheet on how best to sell yourself to this specific person.

Number two, is an inspirational and positive attitude! Someone who has the ability to inspire can build an entire company from the ground up if that is their intention. Passion is the key behind someone who has the ability to inspire. When you have a burning passion within, it shines and radiates through you. Others can feel it and when you tap into that power nothing can stop you from achieving your goals and dreams. If you are truly passionate about and enjoy your work, then it won't seem like work anymore.

The third and final quality is trustworthiness. Now some may think building trust can take a long period of time, even years! But if you have the skill of building rapport quickly with someone, you can build instant trust from the time of the first impression! It all has to do with going back to number one in this list of three, good communication skills, specifically; listening. When you're speaking with someone, look for common ground, similar beliefs, ideals, likes, and even dislikes. When a person thinks you think like them, they'll believe you're a GENIUS!

In reading this short summary of the skill of being able to "Sell" yourself; you'll have obtained a better understanding of why it's important to hone this skill and gained some sense of techniques to use. In doing so, it will ultimately lead to an advantage in the job marketplace or your own business.

How You Can Help Me

We all sell, for instance: I have put hundreds of hours into this book. It has gone thought 12 revisions and several complete rewrites. My goal with this book was not to make money, but to help young adults succeed in the work force. I honestly believe there needs to be a shift of thought to get our country and our world back on track. I think WE are the ones that need to do it. Since I have put a tremendous amount of time and effort into helping you I ask in return that you do a couple small things to help me.

1. Please review my book on Amazon and Goodreads. This is so important to an indie author. I want to be able to help as many people as possible and your reviews help me spread the word so more people hear about this book.

2. Tweet the Daily Show. Here is a pre wrote tweet you can use: @TheDailyShow Bring on mellenials who R helping the world! Invite @IsaacNavias to share his book Holy Shit! Am I Really About to Graduate?

3. Check out my website Jobaftercollege.org. I have a blog and additional movies that will be posted to help you excel at life.

4. Check out what services I offer on my webpage. Most useful to you is that I conduct mock interviews with people over skype to help them overcome their fear and succeed in the interview process. Mention that you have read this book and I will give you half off!

5. Share this book with others who would benefit from it.

6. Write a blog post for me to put on my blog that relates to mellenials

getting jobs. Also if you know any journalists or bloggers let them know about my projects and connect me to them. I would especially like to connect to college papers.

7. Come work for me. I am looking for determined, self motivated college students to help me with my various projects. If you want real life experience while still in college contact me at Inconsulting42@gmail.com

LinkedIn

LinkedIn can be a great way to help you connect and get interviews. I'm sure you will hear all about LinkedIn in school, but they never teach the tricks of how to use it for an end (like getting you the job interview). LinkedIn can also be used as a great way to build your track record.

The first thing is to make sure that your LinkedIn profile looks good. Make sure your picture is up to date. Have your experiences on your profile, including volunteer work and clubs.

Check out this guide for a great walk through for how to set up a stellar profile for new grads: (http://www.onlinecolleges.net/2012/05/07/the-new-networking-ultimate-linkedin-guide-for-2012-grads/).

It is important to note that LinkedIn, like any social media, is constantly changing. While the layout will change numerous times after this book is published the concepts I lay down here have stayed firm since LinkedIn was launched.

Just being on LinkedIn is not going to get you much. The key is to use features on LinkedIn to achieve your ends.

Groups are a great way to network in an interest group and find out what jobs are out there. There are tons of groups out there, and you will be able to find groups that you are already a part of in the real world. Almost every college will have an alumni group (mine is called University at Buffalo Alumni Association). Your alumni chapter should be the first group you join (yes, even while you are still in college). Many times alumni groups will post jobs on the groups that are not posted elsewhere. If you're planning on moving after college, alumni groups can help you meet people in new cities.

So what other groups should you join? Well, my fraternity group has been one of the most useful for me. I have gotten several job interviews from that group, along with meeting a lot of new people when I moved. National college clubs (SHRM, Engineers without borders, toastmasters, etc.) will all have LinkedIn groups. Many cities will have groups. Find groups that you are already connected to somehow, since it will make networking in these groups a lot more effective.

When you go into a group you will see several tabs

Share group | Group rules | Discussions | Members | Promotions | Jobs | Search | More..

Looking though the **discussion tab** can help you find things and see what the group is about. It is common for people to post job opportunities in the Discussion in many groups. There is also a job tab where people who belong to that group can post job openings.

Another very useful tab is the **members tab.** Let's say you want to get a job at Google (good luck). You can go into the members tab and search for Google. Any member in that group that has Google in their profile will pop up. This will help you find people who work in the company you're interested in. When you go to connect to that member you can select that you are in the same group. There is a strong chance that the member will accept your friend request and then you can send them mail though LinkedIn.

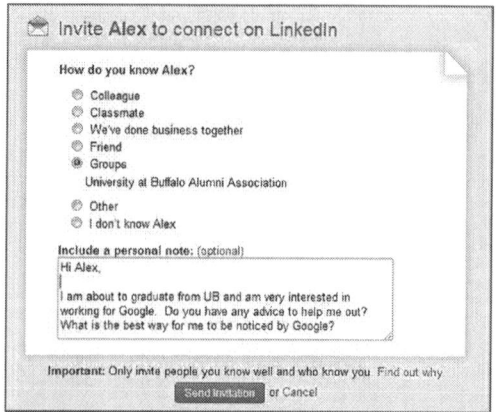

I would start off by asking for suggestions on how to get noticed by that company, or what their experience has been so far with that company. Then move into asking them if they know about any job openings. Once you have built up a relationship with this person, ask them if they can send your resume or refer you to their HR. Getting referred to a company increases your chances of getting hired tenfold. When used correctly, LinkedIn groups can be a useful way to network inside companies and discover what other jobs are out there.

Another way to use LinkedIn is to help you find out more about a company that you are interested in and who you are connected to that works for that company. One of the great things about LinkedIn is if one of your friends is friends with someone you would like to connect to, you can connect with them as well. You just have to ask your friend to be introduced. So to find these types of connections, go to the search (top right), change it to jobs, and type in the company.

So I type in Google and I see

If I click on the 48 people in my network, I find this guy who is a recruiter for Google.

I can then ask my friend, who is friends with him, to introduce me to him. Getting connected to this recruiter though LinkedIn -- and then asking him strategic questions -- will get you way closer to getting a job at Google than just applying for 50 Google jobs online.

LinkedIn can help you find more info about people you want to connect with and help you contact them. Let's say that from your research you find out the name of an HR at a company you are interested in. Unfortunately you don't have their phone number or email address.

You can search for them though LinkedIn. Everyone is going to have different privacy settings on LinkedIn, but many will allow you to see them if you search for them. You can see what groups they are in, and sometimes they even will have their email listed. Even if their profile is mostly private you can still see if you are connected to them somehow. You can also send them a short note though an invite (if you have zero connection to the person you can pick friend and LinkedIn won't ask you to tell them how you are connected).

I met with the assistant director for alumni programs in Syracuse University's Career Services office while writing this book and I wanted to share some of the tips I learned from her.

> 1. She LOVES LinkedIn and thinks it is by far the best social media platform available for networking
>
> 2. You can create a custom URL for your LinkedIn Page by editing your profile. The place to change your URL will be right below your picture. Changing the URL to your name will help with searches and then allows you to put it on your business card and look professional.
>
> 3. LinkedIn now allows people to endorse each other. Getting endorsements will increase your visibility and the amount of people who will visit your page. The easiest ways to get endorsements is to endorse others.
>
> 4. Work your network when you don't need your network!

LinkedIn is the most effective social media platform for networking and jobseekers. Joining groups is an excellent way to connect with people that have common interests. You should immediately join your alumni group and check to see if any of the clubs/fraternities that you are in have groups. Also, look to see what groups are out there that are in the industry you want to go into and start building relationships with people in those groups.

LinkedIn can also be a great way to find more information about someone you want to connect with. It can oftentimes give you contact information that you would have not been able to find otherwise. Of all the social media platforms out there this is the one you should start working on immediately. Make sure you add all of your college friends on LinkedIn as well. It may not help you find a job now, but you never know where your friends will be in 5 years and what connections they will have.

Creative Thinking & Tampons

Creative thinking is something that can help you stand out from the crowd. Creative thinking is looking at a problem and being able to come up with a solution that other people have not thought of. Relatively few people have the ability to approach problems creatively. One of the ways that I have helped myself become more creative is by immersing myself in different cultures.

Different cultures look at problems differently. So when you understand how other cultures think about problems you can look at problems with a different perspective. Studies have also shown that if people have something to work on with their hands during a meeting it helps them use the creative side of their brain. I always have pipe cleaners or Play-Doh at my meetings, which not only helps creativity, but makes the meeting more fun.

Here is a guide on how to increase your creative thinking: http://www.sparringmind.com/creative-thinking/

One night while studying abroad in Australia we were playing the card game "Kings." (By the way, Aussies have never heard of Kings!) Well, the "category" card came up. This is where the person who picks the card gets to choose any category. Everyone has to give answers of things that belong in that category, and then it goes around in a circle until someone messes up.

Well, one girl chose the category "Tampon brands" (which is the only time in my hundreds of Kings games that I have heard someone choose that).

I was fourth in the circle, so I started thinking to myself, "OK, I got: Tampax......Fuck."

Of course someone else said Tampax, so I was thinking like crazy to remember another one before it was my turn. Then I thought, "We're in Australia, there has to be this brand name."

So it got to me and I said, "DownUnder!"

Everyone looked around the circle at each other and were like, "Yeah...yeah, that works."

Creative thinking to the rescue!

Creative thinking is something that many employers look for and is a skill that won't become obsolete. While many of us have never thought about how to increase our creativity (I never had until I wrote this chapter), research has shown that there are ways/exercises you can do to help increase creative thinking.

One such exercise is to restrict yourself. People like to take the path that allows them to think the least. If you restrict the resources available to you that forces you to think outside the box. One of the most famous examples of this is when Dr. Seuss was challenged by his editor to write an entire book using under 50 different words. The result was the famous and beloved *Green Eggs and Ham*. I could point you to many different blogs/guides that talk about creative thinking, but instead I'm going to challenge you to be creative and find them yourselves.

Using College Resources

If your goal is to get a job/career after college, by far the best time to get one is while you're still in college. You will have a much easier time getting a job while you're in college. Once you graduate it becomes a lot more difficult.

Colleges have a ton of resources for you while you're still in school that can help you get a job. A big college statistic that all colleges want to advertise is the percentage of students with a job when they graduate. It makes them look better to prospective students, and increases the chance that you will donate money back to them. You need to be making money for you to donate it don't you?

For these reasons colleges have resources set up to help you get a job. BUT most colleges do an awful job of letting you know what those resources are, so let's look at what they are and how you can find out about them.

Career Resource Center:

Every college/university will have one of these. In many larger universities each school will have one. Go onto your college website and search for the career center. (Or Google your college name and career center.) This is your first step. Set up a time to go talk to a counselor. In that meeting you need to ask them what job services they have and what networking opportunities they have.

Resume/CV reviews:

You bring in your Resume and they critique it. Now the shocking truth is that your resume is one of the least important aspects of getting a good job. At best it will help you get an interview. You do, however, need to make sure that it is not stopping you from getting an interview. So it is still important to have a professional looking resume.

Help with Interviewing:

Most of these centers will have workshops on interviewing. Many colleges will allow you to set up mock interviews with a counselor. They will critique your interview and give you feedback after it is done. This is helpful for improving your interview skills as well as increasing your confidence.

Mentoring program:

Many colleges have a mentoring program where you can get a mentor who is an alumni. This can be great in helping you network and learn more about the real world after college. I have had several great Mentors in my life. Both Jennifer and Nancy, two of my mentors, have helped me tremendously throughout my life. Building a great relationship with a couple of mentors can help you for the rest of your life.

Job and Internship Listing:

Most college have an online database of jobs that companies can post on. Many times the college has a partnership with these companies, and they will look at your resume over some random person's resume. This can be a good way to see what jobs are out there. Remember, although you have a better chance of having your application seen on a college job board, your chance of an interview is still low unless you do follow up.

Job Fairs:

Career resource centers will have a listing of all the job fairs coming to the college. Job fairs can be a great way to network, get your name/resume out there, and get a job. Job fairs thrown by colleges normally have good companies who are looking to hire students attending them. Trust me when I tell you the job fairs outside of college are complete crap. Job fairs can be one of the most useful tools that your college provides you to help you get a job. Make sure you use them. Let's look at how to go about having success at a job fair:

I got my first job after college from a job fair. I was hired by Target to be an executive HR for them (hence many of my awesome tips come from me being on the hiring end of things). I certainly did not get the job right then on the spot, but I did get on their radar. Later I got called into an interview with them because I talked to them at the job fair. There are some things to do to make sure you have success at job fairs.

Stand out!

These recruiters are talking to 200-500 people in one day. Make sure you stand out somehow. For example, when my roommates and I went to a job fair we all had different styles. One roommate would dress up in a suit and tie. He had his resumes ready to hand out and had already looked up who would be at the job fair and how to go about talking to them. He got attention from recruiters because he was professional and prepared.

My other roommate would wing it. He would dress business casual and randomly visit booths to find out what they were about. He got attention because he knew his stuff, and his business card read:

> Ruwan Meepagala
> Fucking Awesome, Inc.
> Creative Consultant

Now I wouldn't suggest your business card saying that, but it worked for him.

So the first thing about standing out is the handshake! When you shake someone's hand, **call them by name** (they will have a name tag on). Use a firm grasp and make eye contact.

For men -- it is best to try and match the grip of the person you're shaking hands with. If you are shaking hands with a woman, don't crush her hand. Be firm and match their grip.

For women -- you want to make sure you have a strong handshake. Practice with friends to make sure your grip is good. No one likes a dead fish handshake.

Next, ask about the job opportunities that they have and see if anything catches your attention. If something does talk to them about it. Find more info for yourself, and tell them why you would be a good fit (how you benefit them; they don't care how it would benefit you to have the job).

When you're done talking to them, ask how to proceed with applying for the job. Give them your resume, thank them for their time, and get their business card. (Call them by their name! "Thanks Bob for talking to me about this job. Here is my resume, do you have a business card? Any hints on what would get me seen when applying? I am really interested in this job"). If they liked you while you talked to them they will give you hints or even say, "Email me when you apply and I will make sure my HR looks at your resume!"

By doing this, you stand out several ways:

1. You called them by name at least twice while talking to them. People LOVE to hear their name. By using it you will stand out and they will feel more connected with you.
2. You told them how their company would benefit from hiring you, instead of talking about what you've done, or how much you want

the job like everyone else.

3. If you have gone to the career center and created a good resume it can help you stand out after the job fair. It also gives them something to help them remember you.

4. You asked them for hints on how to be seen, showing that you understand how business works.

5. After the job fair, if there was a job you were interested in, email that person a thank you note (remember you asked them for their card).

Here's an example of a follow-up email:

Hey Bob,

Thanks for taking the time to talk to me today about the engineering job. It sounds like your company has a great culture! I will let you know when I apply for the engineering job. Thanks again!

Sincerely,

The Man

Job fairs are a great way to meet a real face in the company so you're not just another resume. The contact info you can get, and the impression you can create for an HR in that company can be invaluable. College job fairs can be your best friend if you use them correctly.

Review:

College Career Centers have a lot of useful resources to help you get a job. They will help you with your resume and interviewing skills. They will hold workshops on a variety of topics (how to network, how to dress, etc.). They often have mentoring programs and an online job database. They also will have a list of upcoming job fairs.

College job fairs can be an important way to find out about different companies and jobs. They are also a great place to network and to stand out. They can help put you on that company's radar as well as introduce you to a person in that company that will help you be seen. Make sure you stand out at a job fair, or you won't get much from it.

Magic

Remember that college is a magical place. Make sure that you fully take it in and use the resources available to you. One of the reasons I think college is so awesome is because during my senior year, I lived in a magical house.

I can honestly tell you that some of the funniest moments of your life will come in college. My senior year I lived in my first house and it was a blast. After a couple months of living there, I started to suspect that our house was, in fact, magical. I was kinda kidding at first, but then something so mystical happened that I came to fully believe.

I walked out into the living room the day after we had hosted some drinking games. Ruwan was standing there looking at his fish tank.

"Hey man, do you know where my fish went?"

"It's not in its tank?"

"Nah, I can't find it anywhere."

So we started looking around on the ground for his fish. Nothing.

The fish tank was right next to a drop-off to the first floor. So we went downstairs to see if maybe it had fallen off the landing.

We couldn't find the fish anywhere, but we did find an unopened thirty-rack of Keystones that no one could account for.

So obviously the only explanation was that the fish had gotten out of its tank, fallen to the first floor, and then had morphed into a thirty-rack of Keystones... Yup. Magical.

EQ

While this isn't directly related to getting a job I want to talk about EQ or EI (emotional intelligence) for a second. Amazingly, EQ is barely taught or even mentioned at college. So why should you care about it?

Well for starters there have been many studies showing that IQ (intelligence quotient) does not have a strong correlation with salary. On the other hand, studies have shown that the higher your EQ, the higher your salary is.

The great thing about EQ is that it can be learned. My suggestion is to pick up the book Emotional Intelligence 2.0 by Travis Bradberry. It is a fast and easy read and it will open your eyes and possibly change your life.

Two big keys to help with your EQ:

1. Always call/greet people by their name.

This is so important (and I suck at remembering names). People love to hear their own names. It helps you build an immediate bond with a person you just met if you call them by their name. Now I know how difficult this can be. When I was a freshman in college I dated a girl for about a month without knowing her name.

Yes, I know. One day my roommate came home from class all excited.

"Isaac," he said, "I figured out how you can remember her name! I came up with the perfect rhyme."

"Ok, lay it on me."

"Linguini Shalini!"

Yup. Shalini (Sha-lean-E)... I still to this day remember her name, thanks to the rhyme my roommate made up.

The key to remembering someone's name is to actually try. Then try and associate their name with something that you can remember. You can even ask them if they have a good way to remember their name -- most people have a clever way to remember it. Even though I have real difficulties remembering people's names I now make a conscious effort to remember everyone's name. I have personally seen large dividends from this practice.

2. Active listening.

I didn't even know what this was until my senior year in college. We, as humans, like to talk. When someone is talking to us we are always thinking about what we are going to say next. How can you be really listening if you're thinking about what *you're* going to say?

The key to active listening is to push your thoughts out of your mind and hear what they are saying. After they are done talking, try paraphrasing what they just said. The next step is to be able to identify what emotions the person is feeling.

Active listening can be amazingly powerful and can definitely help you network and build better relationships. Check out *The 7 Habits of Highly Effective People* by Stephen Covey (Habit #5) to get a great break-down and examples of active listening.

I have also created a 15 minute video presentation on EQ on my website at: Jobaftercollege.org

This video will go over even more of the basics to help you with this most important skill.

The Interview

In all honesty, getting the interview is harder than getting the job once you get the interview. Once you have been granted that interview you have gone from a field of 1000+ to maybe around 100. The second interview will bring that down to 10-20. The third interview is normally the top 3 or 4 candidates.

There are some important things to know to give you the edge while interviewing.

The Halo Effect:

This is when the interviewer sees one positive aspect of you that they like and end up evaluating you higher purely from this one attribute.

This could be something as silly as you notice her picture of the yellow lab on her desk. You talk to her for a couple minutes about your yellow lab. She will embellish the other skills you have because of the Halo Effect.

Likeness Effect:

People are drawn to others who are like them. Whether it's that you look similar, or you like the same things, finding ways you are like your interviewer will help you be seen in a positive light. Using similar words and manner of speech that match your interviewer will also increase your likeability.

Attractiveness:

Studies have shown that how attractive you are plays a large factor in influencing people. You may say you can't change your attractiveness, but that is not true. By using proper grooming techniques and dressing appropriately you can increase your attractiveness a great deal.

Males should have a haircut around the time of a big interview. Make sure you have a well-fitting suit with a good color scheme (one where the tie matches the shirt and suit). I have two main interview ensembles I wear. One suit is worn around women (60-70% of HR's are females) who are more likely to be drawn to the color scheme. The other suit is worn more around men, or to really stand out. Remember to wear dress shoes with socks that match your suit.

Women should dress conservatively in a dress, suit (skirt or pant) or a nice blouse with a skirt or slacks depending on the culture of the company. If you wear makeup and/or jewelry keep that to a minimum. Nice shoes (again, conservative low pumps or flats) are a given and stockings may be a good idea.

Men and women should also pay attention to their nails since you'll be shaking hands and perhaps pointing things out to your interviewer.

Behavior based questions:

Did you Know??! (Yes, Bill Nye is the shit). The interview is the worst tool used by companies to determine future job performance! Well, now you know!

Even so, most companies use interviews as their main tools for selection. The big change we have seen in the last 5 years is the emergence of **behavioral based interviews.** Studies have found that behavior based interviews are much better at predicting future job performance.

The theory is that past behavior is likely to be repeated. Any new company will have at least 2 behavior based questions during their interview. The good thing is that there are several behavior based questions that get used a ton so you can already have answers ready when you go into the interview.

It is rare (and a sign of a good interviewer) if I get asked a question that I don't already have an answer for. Let's take a look at the most commonly asked behavior based questions and what we should have in our answers.

Question 1

Tell me about yourself.

This is a common beginning question. While it is not quite a behavior based question, it is so common that we need to cover it. This is also a huge pitfall of a question. If you are not prepared for this one, you may ramble on and add nothing of value. This answer should also be changed based on what each job is looking for.

Don't start talking about your child hood unless it adds something.

When I was applying for an HR position I talked about how my mom and dad got divorced when I was young and how I lived in very different cultures. Because of that, I am great at getting along with all types of people (which is key in HR).

I wouldn't talk about how I had stockpiled over $300 worth of change by the time I was three, since that doesn't add anything. (Whenever I would go into someone's house the first thing I would do is run to the couch and look for change. THERE'S ALWAYS CHANGE!!) I also was a bit of a player. Whenever my dad had people over or brought me to a party I would walk around with two dimes. I would go up to grownups and say, with big two-year-old puppy eyes, "If I had added a nickel I would have a quarter!" Almost always, they gave me a quarter.

When interviewing for a financial job, for example, I might talk about how I earned and managed money at age 2, but would not talk about how my parents lived in different cultures.

So if you are going to talk about your childhood make sure it relates and keep it short. You should then talk about clubs or volunteer events you have done, especially if it relates to the industry/company you are applying to.

Make sure you talk about leadership positions you have had while working for these clubs. For example, for an HR job I would say, "I started a committee in my professional business fraternity based on continuous improvement. One of the first things we realized is that after pledges crossed (went from being pledges to brothers) they would join different cliques and there would be a large disconnect between the brothers. So we set up a brother-to-brother interview program where brothers could choose to sign up and we would pair them with another brother they normally would not get to hang out with. They could do whatever they wanted during that time – seeing a movie, going golfing, whatever.

We had a lot of success with that program. When we first started about ¼ of the brothers signed up. The program got such good feedback that now over 50% the of brothers have signed up.

A lot of you may not have had the opportunity to join a fraternity, but you definitely have had leadership opportunities during college. Think about a time you took leadership in a club, or were a leader in a team project or on a sports team.

This does a ton for me in the interview. I have talked about how I was involved in learning outside of school. I showed that I can take leadership and work within a team. I showed that I care about the well-being of people and am good at organizing events to help people connect (which is big for an HR). Think about *my* answer versus someone who talked randomly about their whole life... Yup, I pwnd them!

You should also talk about any other jobs or experiences you have had that relate to the job you are applying for. It's fine to throw out a couple of your hobbies here too. Hopefully your interviewer will have the same hobby, which will give you the halo effect.

You should expect this question at every single interview and should always have an answer ready that relates to the specific job you are applying for. Practice and time your answer before the interview. The answer should be no longer than 1 or 2 minutes.

Now let's dig into the behavior based questions.

Interviewers are looking for 3 things in your answer.

1. A SPECIFIC **example** relating to the question asked.

2. What **behaviors** you exhibited during the example.

When talking about behaviors exhibited, make sure you are using keywords. Many companies will actually keep tallies on how often you said certain words. They like to hear the words leadership, teamwork, diversity, continuous improvement, communication, culture, problem solving...

3. The **outcome** of the example.

Most people will not tell the outcome of the example, and that docks a lot of points off your answer. Make sure you have good examples where you can speak to good outcomes. When I talked about my brother-to-brother interview program I started, I talked about the starting numbers, how we received great feedback from it, and how the numbers grew to over 50% opting into this program. Those are real, defined numbers that speak to the success of that program and to me as the leader of the program.

Question 2

Tell me about a time you had to work with a team to complete a project. What was the outcome of that project?

Teamwork is extremely important to most companies and they want to make sure that you can work well in a team. You should have 2 or 3 of these examples in your head before you go into any interview. Which example I use depends on the type of position I am applying for. If I am applying for a leadership position I will use an example of when I lead a group with a successful project.

One example I will use is about my junior year in my marketing class when we had a group project where we had to create a new product and market it. I was also pledging a professional business fraternity at the time so I was very busy. I told my group that I would have to miss some meetings because of pledging. After missing a meeting I noticed that my group did nothing when I wasn't there.

I figured then that I could save myself time by taking on the leadership role of the group. Even though this added extra responsibility for me, I am such an effective leader that it would save me and the group time in the long-run. The first thing I did was get to know each of my teammates' strengths and weakness and then instead of splitting the project up evenly like most other groups, I assigned parts that worked to each person's strengths.

I had the artistic ones make the poster and design the packaging. One other teammate and I did the writing, while the other one created the video. Since we were all doing what we were best at, the result was that we finished our project before any other group in the class and we received a 92 on the project, which was the second-highest grade in the class. My teammates also graded me high on the teammate evaluation and I ended up getting at 98 on the project.

That example shows that I can take on a successful leadership position. Now, if I am interviewing for a team member position I am going to give an example of how I worked well in a team when I wasn't the leader.

The key to this answer is:

> 1. Show how you helped your team succeed. Give examples of what YOU personally did to ensure success.
>
> 2. Tell about the outcome. Obviously you want to have an example where the outcome was favorable. Give quantitative data about the outcome (our grade was a 92, we increased performance 50%, ect.). Most people will forget to give the outcome, or just breeze over what the outcome was.

Story Time! This would be an answer NOT to give:

In our freshman year one of my suitemates didn't have a cell phone. We also learned fairly quickly how to break into our suitemate's room though our shared bathroom. So we decided that we would prank my suitemate by changing the time on his clock forward 1 minute every day.

This went on for over a month and a half. Then one day at brunch, Tony was like, "Ya guys, I seem to be getting to class really early lately. I was 45 minutes early for class yesterday. I don't know what's going on!"

We were all trying so hard not to start laughing.

"It just keeps happening. I've been early to everything this whole week!"

Caitlin burst out laughing and Tony found out what we had been doing for the last 45 days.

Question 3

Tell me about one of your weaknesses. Or tell me about a time you made a mistake and how you corrected that mistake.

This can be a make-or-break question. Any good interviewer will know that everyone makes mistakes. It is those who can recognize a weakness or mistake and grow from it that get hired.

When picking a weakness to talk about you want to pick one that is a weakness, but one that you are also working on improving.

Example: Organization has been a weakness of mine for most of my life. When I started working at Target I was missing emails and other information. I found I needed new ways of keeping track of all the information I was receiving.

After trying several different methods, I found that I needed several systems to make sure I recorded all the data that was coming at me. I started keeping two different To-Do sheets: one for my emails, and one for everything else.

I got a planner to record team member scheduling. I started using a desk calendar to track and record longer-term events. After implementing those four systems I was able to get the information flow under control and I stopped missing important data.

Now that I have learned these techniques, whenever I am in a situation where a lot of data is coming at me, I look at creating a system (or several) to allow me to organize all the data. This has helped me tremendously with my organizational skills.

Question 4

Tell me about a time you had to work with a diverse group and how did that change the outcome of the project?

Companies have become increasingly more interested in your ability to work in a diverse group of people. A big reason for this is that studies have found that when diversity is managed well in the work place, there is a large increase in productivity.

People who grow up in different cultures will come up with different solutions to the same problem. When you are able to take the solutions from a variety of different cultures and combine them, you often get an even better solution. That is why companies are so focused on diversity.

When answering this question it is important to identify how working with a diverse group of people helped make the project better.

One example I use is: When I was pledging we had to throw an event for alumni. I had the idea to throw a brunch where we would have pledge-mates from different countries cook their native food. The brunch was a huge hit with the brothers and the alumni.

My pledge class had members from ten different countries and we were able to throw a brunch that had food from all over the world. Not only was it a very successful event because of how tasty and unique the food was, but my pledge brothers and I learned a ton about cooking from different countries.

Here is my favorite diversity story, but as you will see it is clearly not an answer to an interview question.

My sophomore year in college I did a study abroad in Australia. I lived in the international apartments so I had friends from all around the world living next to me. The first week we were there, we had a party over at my buddy Dane's apartment. Dane, who is a white Canadian dude, passed out on his own couch before midnight.

I was like, "Guys, we need to draw on this dude. His shoes are on and everything."

My Kenyan buddy Kevin was like, "I got something, I'll be right back."

So he went up to grab something to draw on Dane with. He came back a few minutes later with a tube of toothpaste. All the Kenyans got excited and crowded around Dane. They started drawing penises and stuff on his face with toothpaste.

I was just standing there thinking, "What is going on, why the fuck are they using toothpaste?"

...and then it hit me. Many Kenyans have really really dark skin, so marker doesn't show up on their skin. Instead, they toothpaste each other.

So Dane woke up about 30 minutes later. He started stretching, then slowly put his right hand onto his face. He pulled it off quickly and looked at it, looking confused and disgusted.

"Uuua Eye... WHAT IS THIS WHITE STICKY STUFF ALL OVER

MY FACE?"

Creating your own Job

While this book focuses on how to get a job in a company I want to leave you with another possibility. We are seeing the emergence of the small business again in America. Many of these entrepreneurs are baby boomers who have great skills and experience but have been laid off. There is a lot of opportunity for people our age to help baby boomers run their small businesses.

A key skill we have is our deep understanding of technology. We grew up almost our whole lives with computers and the internet. We were still at a young age when the mobile market took off and changed the way we live and work. These things are part of any millennium. Baby boomers often struggle with the technology part of business and this is a key skill we can utilize. Some of the most marketable skill sets for our age are: Wordpress Design/Management, Social Media, SEO, Online Marketing, Photo Shop and Photography. If you can develop one of these skills you have the ability to make money consulting. I have created a whole company around helping small entrepreneurs succeed. Even if you want to get a traditional job doing this type of consulting work can be a great way to make extra money while searching.

We are also seeing more and more young people create their own companies. While many are doing various types of consulting, others are being creative and finding ways to create products that are not out there, or are finding better ways to get products out there.

In the last month I have met a bunch of 20-30 year olds who have started their own companies. One is creating dog treats from the leftover food from college dining halls. Another started a company reviewing movies, focusing on indie or non-main stream movies. I've worked with an up-and-coming rapper from NYC and am partnering with a marriage counselor to create a health care consulting company. I'm working with a young author who has had enough success with her self-published books that she was able to leave her full time job. I have several friends who have started their own photography companies. I could go on and on with all the young adults I've meet that have been able to create their own jobs.

While it is not easy to create your own company or job, it is now a definite possibility. The internet has made it so that you can start up and market a business with almost no investment money. All you need is a solid plan, creativity, an understanding of how to use your creativity with technology and most importantly, the will power and discipline to succeed.

Whichever path you choose you are already a step ahead of most of your peers just by reading this book. While following the strategies laid out in the book will not be easy, they will be far more effective at getting you the job you want.

You now know how to network your way into a job by using strategies like volunteering, utilizing clubs and fraternities, and building relationships with professors and academic advisers. You know how to use LinkedIn, which is by far the most effective Social Media networking platform. You know that getting referred to a company is more effective than just applying online, and you know techniques to help you get referred. You have learned how to use your College Career Center to the fullest. Finally, you are now more prepared for the interview and the questions they are going to throw at you.

Be confident that while getting a great job is harder now than ever before, it is still most certainly possible. If you use these techniques to network and been seen you will have the success you want. Good luck, and may the Force be with you!

The End

Extra Resources

My goal with this book is to give to the basic information to help you have success after college. I kept this book short on purpose, because of that I wanted to provide other resources that can give you more information on topics you are more interested in learning about.

EQ:

Emotional Intelligence 2.0 by Travis Bradberry and Jean Greaves:

I recommend this book to everyone no matter what your major or goal in life is. Fast read and could change your life.

The Definitive Book of Body Language by Barbara Pease, Allan Pease

Business:

Think and Grow Rich by Napoleon Hill:

This one of the most powerful books I have ever read. I recommend this book to everyone, no matter what your career is.

Good to Great by Jim Collins:

Very interesting book that really looks at how to create a better company. A good read for anyone looking to go into management.

The 7 Habits of Highly Effective People by Stephen R. Covey

Glassdoor.com:

This is another excellent resource to use. It lets you look at how workers are rating their company. It shows you salaries of different positions, and they even have interview questions sometimes. Definitely check out this website before you go in for the interview, or to find places to work that fit the culture you want to work in.

LinkedIn:

Great online guide: http://www.onlinecolleges.net/2012/05/07/the-new-networking-ultimate-linkedin-guide-for-2012-grads/

People to Follow:

Dr John Sullivan: Is a HR thought leader and has a lot of great articles online.

Endnotes

1. http://www.cleveland.com/business/index.ssf/2012/04/half_of_recent_college_grads_u.html

2. http://www.nydailynews.com/news/money/college-grads-find-full-time-work-study-shows-article-1.1075873

3. http://www.ere.net/2012/05/07/10-compelling-numbers-that-reveal-the-power-of-employee-referrals/

4. http://www.umkc.edu/getinvolved/fsa-national-statistics.asp

5. http://www.usatodayeducate.com/staging/index.php/campuslife/examining-the-benefits-of-greek-life

Made in the USA
Lexington, KY
13 December 2016